W9-AEM-164

Drug Abuse and Society™

CAFFEINE AND NICOTINE
A Dependent Society

ROSEN
PUBLISHING®

New York

Heather Hasan

To my nephew, Drew, with love

Published in 2009 by The Rosen Publishing Group, Inc.
29 East 21st Street, New York, NY 10010

First Edition

Library of Congress Cataloging-in-Publication Data

Hasan, Heather.
Caffeine and nicotine: a dependent society / Heather Hasan.
    p. cm.—(Drug abuse and society)
Includes bibliographical references.
ISBN-13: 978-1-4358-5015-6 (library binding)
1. Caffeine—Juvenile literature. 2. Caffeine habit—Juvenile literature.
3. Nicotine—Juvenile literature. 4. Tobacco use—Juvenile literature.
I. Title.
HV5809.5.H37 2009
613.8'4—dc22

                                                    2008010294

Manufactured in Malaysia

Contents

INTRODUCTION

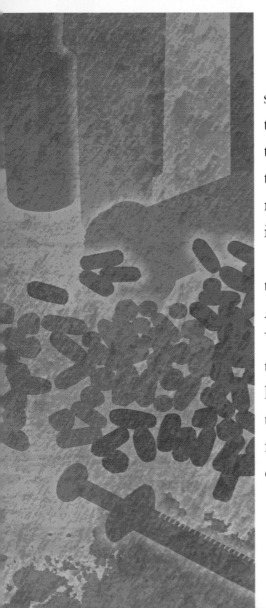

Nicotine is a colorless, oily liquid that is found in the leaves of the tobacco plant. It can be poisonous, so it protects the tobacco plant from insects that would otherwise eat it. Nicotine is also the drug that people get addicted to when they smoke or chew tobacco. However, nicotine is just as harmful to humans as it is to insects.

Tobacco kills more people each year than cocaine, heroin, crack, suicide, alcohol, AIDS, and automobile accidents combined. Yet every day, three thousand young people try smoking for the first time. Of these kids, thirty will die in traffic accidents and twenty-three will be murdered. However, a far greater number, 750, will die a premature death as a result of tobacco use.

Smoking while drinking a cup of coffee could cause more damage to the heart than either act by itself.

Caffeine, on the other hand, is the most commonly used drug in America. More than 90 percent of Americans use this drug every day, mainly by consuming coffee, tea, and chocolate. It is also added to sodas and energy drinks. Caffeine is found naturally in many different kinds of plants. Because it is found so abundantly in nature, it has been used in food and drinks for centuries. Plants contain caffeine in their fruits, seeds, and leaves because it helps protect them from attack by fungi and bacteria. Caffeine, like nicotine, can be poisonous and acts as a mild insecticide, helping the plants to grow.

Caffeine and nicotine are common. They are used by millions of people every day. They are even sold in stores. However, that does not mean that they are safe.

Many people forget that caffeine and nicotine are drugs. However, caffeine and nicotine indeed are drugs. Like any other drugs, they have the potential to do harm. Like other drugs, caffeine and nicotine change the way that the mind and the body work. They alter the way that people think, feel, and act. It is these effects that first drew people to these drugs and made them as popular as they are today.

CHAPTER 1
Caffeine, Nicotine, and American Culture

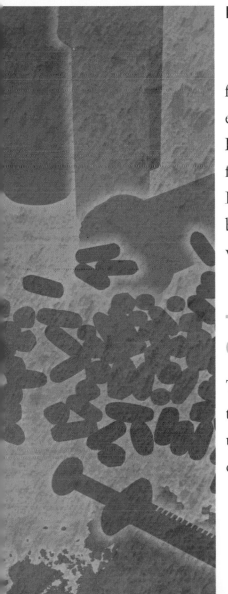

The emergence of many drugs, including caffeine and nicotine, in American culture began with the fifteenth- and sixteenth-century European explorers such as Christopher Columbus. During Columbus's time, there were very few mind-altering substances available in Europe. European explorers therefore brought mind-altering substances home with them whenever possible.

THE HISTORY OF CAFFEINE

The main sources of caffeine are the beans of the coffee plant, tea leaves, the kola nut (once used to flavor colas), and the pods from the cocoa plant (used to make chocolate). Coffee

The football-shaped pods shown here are cocoa fruits. Cocoa fruits contain the seeds that will become cocoa beans. Cocoa beans are used to make chocolate.

has been around at least as far back as 850 CE. At that time, the people of Africa chewed coffee beans, which are the berries of the coffee plant. Later, people made wine steeped with coffee beans. Finally, coffee beans were roasted, ground up, and steeped in hot water. Coffee plants were taken from Africa to southern Arabia and reached the Middle East in the 1200s. In the 1500s, coffee was introduced to Europe, and it had reached North America by the 1600s. Coffee plants are now grown in tropical countries around the world.

Tea has been around even longer than coffee. The Chinese drank tea as far back as five thousand years ago. The use of tea spread from China to Japan around 600 CE. Dutch traders then brought the idea of tea drinking from East Asia to Europe in the 1600s. Soon after that, tea drinking was introduced to North

America. America made tea drinking even easier when tea bags were invented in 1904.

Like the coffee bean and the tea leaf, the kola nut was known by the ancients. It is still chewed in some West African cultures because of its stimulatory effects. The kola nut was once widely used to flavor sodas. The first cola drink was invented by a pharmacist in Georgia in the 1880s. To make the syrup for his drink, he used kola nuts, coca leaves, citrus, and cinnamon. Though most commercial soft drinks are no longer flavored with kola nuts, a significant amount of caffeine is now added to cola products.

The Winston Man

David Goerlitz appeared as a model in forty-two advertisements for Winston cigarettes in the 1980s. He began smoking when he was fifteen, and, at his worst, Goerlitz smoked three and a half packs of cigarettes a day. Even before he got out of bed each morning, Goerlitz began smoking, and it was the last thing he did at night. At age thirty-four, while acting as a stuntman for Harrison Ford in the movie *Witness*, half of Goerlitz's body suddenly went numb. He had had a stroke. However, Goerlitz was not persuaded to quit smoking until he saw twelve- and thirteen-year-old children smoking and realized that he had played a part in influencing them to start. Goerlitz stopped smoking at age thirty-nine and quit his job as the Winston Man, walking away from a lot of money. Goerlitz took a historic stand against tobacco companies in 1988, condemning them for targeting America's youth. He now travels throughout the country, persuading young people not to smoke.

CAFFEINE AND AMERICAN CULTURE

Coffee is the number one source of caffeine in America. According to the National Coffee Association, more than 50 percent of Americans drink coffee daily. Almost every place that sells food in the United States also sells coffee, from gourmet restaurants to fast-food chains. Coffee is often at the center of social situations. People socialize with a cup of coffee. Coffee is also a symbol of hospitality. It is often the first thing a guest will be offered when visiting. In fact, many consider it rude if coffee is not offered after a meal.

More than 90 percent of coffee in America is consumed in the morning. Caffeine has become an acceptable means to get Americans going in the morning, which is reflected in advertisements such as "The best part of waking up is Folgers in your cup." Other commercials claim that coffee boosts your ambition and helps you to succeed. Energy drinks, described as coffee for the new generation, are very popular with young people in today's society. They can contain as much as two to four times more caffeine than coffee. Energy drinks, like Red Bull and Rockstar, target teens by promising weight loss, higher energy, and a legal high. According to Simmons Research, 31 percent of teens say they drink energy drinks. The wide acceptance of caffeine as a way to enhance performance and control behavior could be dangerous.

In America, almost every place that serves food also sells coffee, as shown here in this New York sandwich shop.

THE HISTORY OF NICOTINE

No one knows exactly when tobacco was first used or how people learned to grow it. However, long before Europeans came to America, Native Americans were growing and using it. When Christopher Columbus visited San Salvador in the West Indies in 1492, he noticed Native Americans smoking and chewing tobacco and inhaling it through their noses. The type of tobacco that is inhaled is called snuff. In 1607, British settlers founded Jamestown, the first New World colony. These settlers survived by growing tobacco and shipping it to England. Tobacco became so important in the New World that it even replaced money as currency for a while. People used tobacco to cover the cost of building churches and to pay ministers for marriages and funerals.

In the late 1700s, snuff was made fashionable in America by the wealthy and important. Etiquette was developed for how to handle a snuff box, how to hold snuff, and how to inhale it. Cigarettes did not become the main tobacco product in America until the mid–1920s, but smoking soon became the "in" thing to do. As early as the 1920s, smoking was glamorized in the movies. Actresses smoking in the movies were portrayed as confident and independent. Handsome male stars who smoked were shown to be suave, rugged, and manly. From the beginning, smoking was also closely connected to sex. Since sex was forbidden to

RED CLOUD.

Chewing Tobacco.

This 1867 tobacco ad shows a Native American. Long before Europeans came to America, Native Americans grew and used tobacco.

be shown in films, smoking was used to represent it. Tobacco industries even used to regularly pay movie studios to show their products in films.

NICOTINE AND AMERICAN CULTURE

We now know beyond a reasonable doubt that tobacco use causes addiction, disease, and death. Though cigarette smoking used to be commonplace in American culture, it is no longer considered to be as socially acceptable. Most Americans dislike smoking, and even regular smokers wish they could quit. However, Americans tolerate smoking because it has been a part of our culture for so long.

However, the tobacco industry has the incentive to encourage smoking. According to the Federal Trade Commission, in 2003, tobacco companies spent more than 15.1 billion dollars to market their products in America. The age groups that these companies target are children and young adolescents. They know of the National Institute on Drug Abuse's findings that nearly 90 percent of smokers start smoking before the age of eighteen. The amount of smoking in youth-oriented films has increased by 50 percent since 1998. These films give adolescents the perception that smoking is acceptable or even fashionable. Many studies have shown that teens who watch their favorite actors light up on screen are enticed to try smoking themselves. A report in the *Lancet*, a medical journal, in 2003 stated that smoking in movies is responsible for the addiction of more than one thousand teens in the United States every day. Teens should know that while they are being entertained, they are also being advertised to and manipulated by an industry that is not concerned with their health or well-being.

Nicotine is considered by the American Medical Association to be a gateway drug for teens, meaning that it is linked to future or simultaneous substance abuse. A 2007 report by Columbia

Here, a young advocate is protesting Hollywood's silence and lack of action against the presence of smoking in youth-related films.

University's National Center for Addiction and Substance Abuse found that teens who smoke are five times more likely to drink and are thirteen times more likely to use marijuana than those who don't smoke.

Myths and Facts About Caffeine

Myth: Caffeine makes you more alert.
Fact: Increased heartbeat and respiration can lead people to believe that they are more alert. However, caffeine actually decreases reaction time.

Myth: Caffeine consumption is no big deal.
Fact: The need that people feel for their morning cup of coffee is usually more than just a habit. It's an addiction. If it were simply a habit, those who regularly drink coffee, cola, or energy drinks could stop or switch to decaffeinated forms without experiencing negative effects. Yet, people do notice a difference in the way they feel.

Myth: Caffeine does not have serious effects on the body.
Fact: Long-term effects of caffeine use include ulcers, breast disease, and heart disease. Dr. Jim Lane at the Duke University Medical School has shown that the amount of caffeine that many Americans ingest each day can raise their blood pressure enough to increase their chances of having a heart attack or stroke by 20 to 30 percent. Also, lack of sleep because of caffeine can cause permanent changes to teens' developing brains.

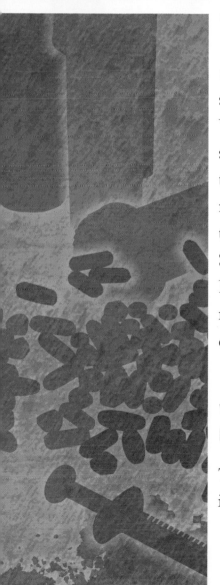

CHAPTER 2

Users and Pushers

I t is pretty safe to say that most American teens today are well aware of the dangers of drug use. The dangers of substance abuse are preached everywhere. With all the warnings, why are dangerous substances still so appealing to teens? More than three thousand young people become regular smokers each day. That's more than one million new smokers each year. Sadly, the Centers for Disease Control and Prevention (CDC) has concluded that five million children who are alive today will die prematurely from smoking.

WHY TEENS START USING NICOTINE

The human body makes it quite clear that it does not like, need, or want tobacco

Many teens start smoking because their friends smoke. They may see smoking as a way to rebel or assert their independence.

smoke. First-time smokers have reported burning sensations in their throats, choking, dizziness, and nausea. So, why do so many teens ignore good advice and even their own bodies and begin this deadly practice?

Research states that peer acceptance is a major reason why so many adolescents start smoking. During adolescence, teens assert their independence and seek out their identity, but they still crave the approval and acceptance of their friends. If teens hang out with smokers, they are much more likely to start smoking themselves. According to a study done by Philip Morris USA in 2004, two-thirds of smokers from age eleven to seventeen say they got their first cigarette from a friend. Teens don't want to feel like outsiders, but the truth these days is that not everyone is smoking. The number of young people that smoke is decreasing. In fact, fewer than 20 percent of teenagers smoke regularly.

Family influence also plays a big part in whether a teenager starts smoking. Research in child development has repeatedly shown that parents are the biggest influences in their children's lives. Teens whose parents do not smoke are the least likely to try smoking. Studies done by the U.S. Department of Health and Human Resources and the Philip Morris tobacco company have shown that kids who have a parent who smokes is at least twice as likely to take up smoking. Having an older brother or sister who smokes makes a child three times as likely to start smoking. However, kids whose parents talk to them regularly about not smoking are less likely to smoke (even if their parents smoke). It helps for teens to know that most adults would not start smoking if they could do it again. It also helps for parents to tell their teens how difficult it is to quit smoking.

Nicotine products are easy to get and easy to use, and they are legal. The ease of obtaining cigarettes adds to the number of teens who abuse them. Many young smokers get older kids to buy their cigarettes for them. Others steal them from their parents, older siblings, or retail stores. Still others are able to purchase nicotine products for themselves. According to the CDC, about 70 percent of middle school students in 2004 were not asked to show proof of age when purchasing cigarettes. It is also somewhat easy for minors to buy cigarettes online. A study published in the *Journal of the American Medical Association* states that children were able to successfully purchase cigarettes online 92 percent of the time that they tried.

A lack of understanding also contributes to teenage nicotine abuse. Many teens are being misinformed by their friends, who are more than happy to assure them that the risks are minimal. Even though most teens have heard that prolonged tobacco use can cause health problems such as cancer and emphysema and eventually lead to death, it is often hard for them to grasp such long-term consequences. However, adolescents should understand that smoking is also affecting their lives now.

THE PSYCHOLOGICAL EFFECTS
OF NICOTINE ABUSE

The nicotine that is found in tobacco products is a psychoactive drug, or one that acts on the central nervous system, where it alters brain function. Nicotine is absorbed through the skin, through the lining of the nose and mouth, or in the lungs. Once it enters the bloodstream, it takes just seconds for the nicotine to

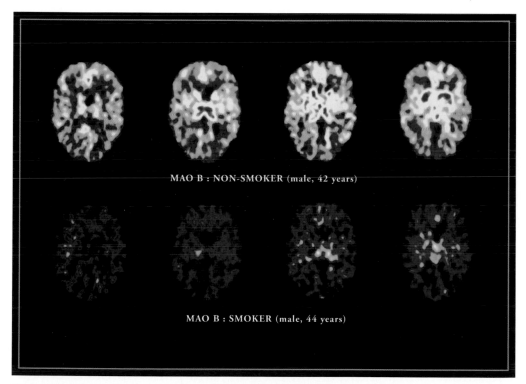

MAO B : NON-SMOKER (male, 42 years)

MAO B : SMOKER (male, 44 years)

These brain scans show the levels of MAO B in the brains of nonsmokers (*top*) and smokers (*bottom*). The scans show that smokers have much less MAO B in their brains than nonsmokers.

reach the brain. Nicotine acts on the brain, causing changes in perception, mood, consciousness, and behavior.

Nicotine increases levels of dopamine in parts of the brain, producing feelings of pleasure and reward. Dopamine, a molecule sometimes referred to as the "pleasure molecule," is also the chemical responsible for addictions to cocaine and heroin. People continue smoking so they can feel these pleasant feelings. Smokers also associate smoking with pleasurable things, like special occasions, an after-dinner "treat," talking on the phone, or as a way to relax. According to the U.S. Department of Health and Human Services, tobacco use in adolescents has also been linked to behaviors such as fighting, possession of weapons, engaging in risky sexual behavior, and the use of alcohol and other drugs.

HEALTH EFFECTS OF NICOTINE

Nicotine is a poison. In fact, just a tiny drop of pure nicotine could kill a grown man in a matter of minutes. For this reason, nicotine has actually been used as an insecticide. Though using nicotine-containing drugs such as cigarettes or chewing tobacco may not kill a person instantly, they are very harmful to people's health. Upon smoking, the nicotine in cigarettes immediately speeds up the smoker's heartbeat, blood pressure, and pulse. Smokers cough more and produce more phlegm.

Teen smokers get sick more often than nonsmokers, and when they get a cold, they are more likely to develop respiratory illnesses, like bronchitis and pneumonia. Smoking also decreases the physical fitness of teens and makes asthmatic conditions worse. Smoking can even retard the lung growth of smoking teens. Teen smokers tend to have worse lung function and weaker hearts. This will greatly hinder sports activities. In addition to that, smoking causes wrinkles, stains the teeth, and gives smokers bad breath. Smokers are also three times more likely to develop cavities than nonsmokers.

Long-term use of tobacco products increases the risk of heart disease, including strokes, heart attacks, and aneurysms. According to the U.S. surgeon general, 18 percent of deaths from heart disease are caused by smoking. Nicotine use also causes cancer. It is associated with cancers of the mouth, esophagus, pharynx, larynx, kidneys, stomach, pancreas, bladder, ureter, and cervix. Foremost among cancers caused by tobacco use is lung cancer. According to the CDC, 90 percent of lung cancer deaths can be directly attributed to smoking.

THE PSYCHOLOGICAL EFFECTS OF CAFFEINE

Caffeine, like nicotine, is a psychoactive drug. Because caffeine affects the brain and the nerves, it can affect a person's mood and behavior. However, the effect varies with different people and also depends on the amount of caffeine consumed. Children and teens are at a much greater risk of experiencing side effects than

A lot of people use caffeine to get them going in the morning. However, too much caffeine can cause a person to feel irritable, jittery, anxious, lightheaded, and nervous.

adults are because of their smaller size. A small or moderate amount of caffeine usually elevates the mood of the consumer. However, too much caffeine causes irritability, jitters, anxiety, lightheadedness, and nervousness. Caffeine's pleasurable effects are also short-lived. When it wears off, it leaves people feeling tired and let down.

It is well known that caffeine can affect a person's sleep. Most people who consume caffeine before going to bed find it harder to go to sleep, and they may wake up several times during the night. In general, those who drink large amounts of coffee (or smoke) get less sleep than those who don't. Lack of sleep can be harmful to teens. It affects their ability to pay attention in class, which can hurt their grades. It can also affect a teen's ability to do well in sports. Lack of sleep can also negatively affect a person's mood. Some researchers even believe that lack of sleep can cause permanent changes in a child's developing brain. However, not much is known about caffeine's mental effects in the long term.

How Much Caffeine Are You Consuming?

Many people do not realize how much caffeine they are consuming. The American Dietetic Association recommends that adults consume only 200–300 milligrams of caffeine per day, and most experts recommend that teens consume not more than 100 mg per day. However, most people get a lot more than that. Caffeine is not only in coffee and tea, but it is found in energy drinks, diet pills, over-the-counter pain pills, and chocolate. Here are some common products and the amount of caffeine they contain (as listed by the Mayo Clinic):

Product	Amount of Caffeine (mg)
Starbucks Coffee Grande, 16 oz	330
Plain, Brewed Coffee, 8 oz	95
Green Tea, Brewed, 8 oz	30–50
Snapple Iced Tea, 16 oz	18
7 Up, 12 oz	0
Diet Coke, 12 oz	47
Mountain Dew, 12 oz	54
SoBe No Fear, 16 oz	174
No Name (Formally Known as Cocaine), 8.4 oz	280
Hershey's Special Dark Chocolate Bar, 1.45 oz	16
Häagen-Dazs Coffee Ice Cream, 1/2 cup	30
Excedrin, Extra Strength, 2 tablets	130
NoDoz Maximum Strength, 1 tablet	200

THE HEALTH EFFECTS OF CAFFEINE

The main reason that most people use caffeine products is to wake them up and give them a feeling of alertness. Like nicotine, caffeine is also a stimulant. As a stimulant, caffeine increases the heart rate, raises blood pressure, and increases the breathing rate. Even moderate amounts of caffeine can be dangerous for people who have conditions such as cardiovascular disease, high blood

Young adults spend billions of dollars each year purchasing energy drinks like the ones shown here. There are hundreds of energy drinks on the market today.

pressure, and anxiety. Though toxicity of caffeine occurs only at very high doses, it is usually teenagers who overconsume it.

A story in the *Taipei Times* told of an eighteen-year-old boy who was rushed to the hospital with sudden heart arrhythmia. The teen had been drinking eight 16-ounce cans of Rockstar energy drinks each night. He had no idea that drinking that much caffeine could harm him. In fact, most of the energy drinks that are so popular among teens do not even disclose how much caffeine they contain. An article in the *New York Times* in 2006 stated that a survey conducted by researchers at Northwestern University found that between the years 2001 and 2004, 250 reports were made to the Illinois Poison Control Center concerning overdoses of caffeine. The caffeine was ingested in several forms, including dietary supplements, medications, and energy drinks. The average age of those overdosed was twenty-one.

Caffeine abuse can cause palpitations, tremors, insomnia, diarrhea, nausea, vomiting, chest pains, sweating, and neurological symptoms. Unfortunately, there has been little scientific research done on how large amounts of caffeine intake can affect adolescents over time.

CHAPTER 3
Human Behavior and Addiction

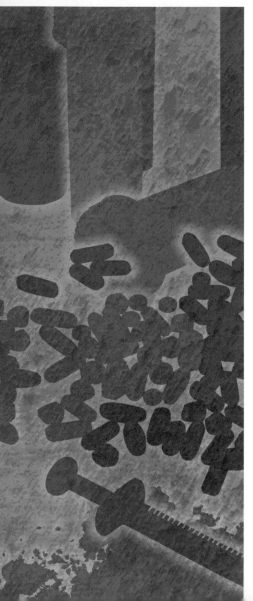

Gruen Von Behrens was thirteen and on a camping trip when one of his friends took out a can of chewing tobacco that he had stolen from his father's dresser drawer. Like too many other teenagers, Von Behrens tried the tobacco because he wanted to fit in. It made him feel sick and dizzy, but he continued to use it. Soon, what started out as an attempt to be cool was the beginning of an addiction that would affect Von Behrens's life in unimaginable ways.

By the time he was fourteen years old, Von Behrens was hooked on nicotine. Soon, he was using more than half a can of chewing tobacco a day. Chewing tobacco seemed harmless to Von Behrens. Like Von Behrens, a lot of kids think that smokeless tobacco is a good alternative to cigarettes because no smoke is being inhaled. However, Von Behrens was wrong. It did not take long for him to get sick. When he was sixteen, he noticed a small white spot on his tongue. This spot grew, and soon Von Behrens's speech was slurring and he was drooling. A trip to the dentist confirmed that he had cancer. Von Behrens had squamous cell carcinoma. Going into his first surgery, he was given a 25 percent chance of survival. Both he and his mother were devastated.

Von Behrens, a good-looking boy, underwent dozens of surgeries in which half his neck muscles, his lymph nodes, his lower teeth and jawbone, and half of his tongue were removed. He survived, but he greatly regrets his decision to use tobacco. He now works for the National Spit Tobacco Education Program, warning young audiences to stay away from nicotine products. Nicotine causes cancer no matter how it gets into the body. "If I had known then what I know now," Von Behrens says, "I never would have put a dip in my mouth."

WHAT IS ADDICTION?

People use drugs for many different reasons, and they become addicted for many different reasons as well. Addiction is complicated, and understanding it can be a very difficult thing to do. Even many drug abusers do not understand the nature of their own addictions. According to the National Institute on Drug

People continue smoking despite the negative effects to their health because of the feelings of pleasure and euphoria that the drugs in the cigarettes give them.

Abuse, "Addiction is characterized by compulsive drug seeking and use, even in the face of negative health consequences."

Few people start using a drug with the intention of getting addicted to it. However, no matter why a person begins using a mood-altering drug, most come back because of the feelings of pleasure and euphoria that the drug gives them. Nicotine's and caffeine's ability to reward people with pleasurable feelings is key to their addictive nature. Many, like Gruen Von Behrens, begin using a chemical substance with the idea that they will try it only once. Von Behrens liked the way the nicotine made him feel, so he used it more. Eventually, people develop a tolerance for the chemical substance they are using. Tolerance is a process by which a person's body becomes used to the drug so that it no longer has the same pleasurable effect. The person uses more and more of the drug in order to reach the desired feelings.

PHYSICAL DEPENDENCE ON NICOTINE AND CAFFEINE

Drug addicts are dependent upon, or controlled by, the drug(s) that they use. Nicotine disrupts the normal system that the brain uses to coordinate its many activities. Physical dependence on nicotine results when the brain makes adjustments to restore the balance of activity in the presence of nicotine. Once this happens, the brain needs the nicotine to maintain balance. In its absence, everything is out of whack. Research shows that this readjusting of the brain occurs very quickly in children. Mayo Clinic researchers report that children who have smoked only a few cigarettes experience the same symptoms of nicotine addiction as adults who smoke heavily.

Once addicted, a person continues using a chemical substance to avoid the affects of withdrawal. For nicotine, the physical symptoms of withdrawal include irritability, headaches and dizziness, increased appetite, trouble sleeping, and difficulty

Some of the withdrawal symptoms of nicotine and caffeine include irritability, headaches, trouble sleeping, and difficulty thinking and staying focused.

thinking and staying focused. For someone attempting to stop nicotine use, it generally takes a few weeks to a few months for these symptoms to subside.

Caffeine, like nicotine, is an addictive substance. As with nicotine, a person who regularly uses caffeine will develop a tolerance for it and require higher doses to achieve the desired effect. People form a physical dependence on caffeine rather quickly, usually within a couple of weeks or months with regular use. A person addicted to caffeine will experience withdrawal if he or she stops using it. The withdrawal symptoms of caffeine include anxiety, depression, difficulty sleeping and concentrating, irritability, headaches, and nausea. In general, the more caffeine consumed, the more severe the withdrawal symptoms usually are. The body's physical dependence on a drug is not the only factor that determines a person's likelihood of becoming an addict. How vulnerable a person is to addiction is very complicated. Psychological factors, personality traits, environmental factors, genetics, and the characteristics of the drug itself all contribute to addiction.

THE PSYCHOLOGY OF ADDICTION

Psychological factors play a large role in the development of addiction. Mood-altering drugs can be very tempting to people who suffer from chronic depression or anxiety, putting them at a higher risk for developing an addiction. This is exemplified by the fact that many become addicted to drugs while serving in wars. The U.S. Veterans Affairs documented a significant rise in drug use by soldiers in Iraq due to the daily stress they are under. Sadly enough, during World War I and World War II, soldiers were given free cigarettes by the American Red Cross, the YMCA, and the Salvation Army, as well as tobacco companies themselves. Soldiers that went to war as nonsmokers often came home addicted to cigarettes. Studies have also shown that the incidence of smoking is higher for people that suffer from other mental illnesses, such as bipolar disorder and schizophrenia. In fact, studies have shown that as many as 90 percent of people suffering from schizophrenia smoke.

Once a person is addicted to nicotine, he or she grows used to the psychological effects of it. When a person feels that he or she needs a drug to feel "normal," that person is experiencing psychological dependence on that drug. Many smokers can think of nothing else but cigarettes after they have gone without smoking for a while. In addition to the physical withdrawal explained earlier, people attempting to give up smoking also experience a kind of psychological withdrawal. For some, the sight, smell, and feel of cigarettes or coffee and the rituals that go along with their use make quitting even more difficult. Nicotine users get used to certain rituals, like smoking after meals, in certain places, or under certain levels of stress. Caffeine users may drink coffee to get them going in the morning, drink coffee with meals, or consume energy drinks while studying. In order to

During World War I and World War II, soldiers were often given free cigarettes. Because of this, many soldiers who went to war as nonsmokers came home addicted to cigarettes.

quit, it is sometimes necessary for a person to change the behaviors that he or she associates with the particular drug.

The concept of "addictive personality" is controversial among researchers. This idea proposes that people abuse drugs because of their underlying personalities. Though the notion of addictive personality has largely been rejected, many researchers list certain personality traits that predict addiction to chemical substances. Risk takers, people who have poor self-control, and people who have a low tolerance for stress are at an increased risk for developing an addiction. Scientists, like Richard Grucza, an epidemiologist at Washington University School of Medicine, believe that traits such as these affect the way that

Symptoms of Addiction

Teenagers often do not see a link between their actions today and the consequences that will affect them later in life. However, according to the CDC, the younger a person is when he or she starts smoking, the more likely it will become an addiction and continue into adulthood. Here are some signs that you might be addicted to nicotine:

- You alter your plans so that you can smoke.
- When you haven't had a cigarette in a while, you get anxious, irritable, tired, you have trouble concentrating, or you get a headache.
- You continue smoking even when you're sick.
- You've tried unsuccessfully to quit.

a person responds to other risk factors such as environmental factors and genetics.

ENVIRONMENTAL AND GENETIC FACTORS AFFECTING ADDICTION

Environmental factors can include the availability of a substance and its acceptance as a social drug in the culture. As was discussed in chapter 2, both caffeine and nicotine are quite accessible in America. Caffeine is legal for people of all ages, and it is a very accepted drug in American society. In fact, caffeine is often not even thought of as a drug. Though the use of nicotine is illegal for individuals under the age of eighteen, kids are generally able to easily obtain it. Though most Americans dislike smoking, nicotine is not looked upon with as much stigma as other illegal drugs, like marijuana or cocaine.

There are biological differences in people that make some people more prone to drug addiction. Scientists will never find just one gene responsible for addiction. It is the result of many interacting genes. These genes can give a person a vulnerability to addiction in different settings or situations. According to Dr. Glen R. Hanson, professor of pharmacology and toxicology at the University of Utah and the acting director of the National Institute on Drug Abuse, genetics may be responsible for a person starting drug use. Genetics may also be responsible for how much of a "reward" a person gets while using a drug. For instance, a particular drug may make one person sick while it gives another person pleasure. Dr. Hanson also believes that genetics might be a factor in addiction because genes are responsible for making some people better at making decisions, even at a young age. It is important for young people to know that just because they have a genetic predisposition to addiction, they are not doomed. Everyone has the ability to make choices. These kids should use knowledge to their advantage.

Ten Great Questions to Ask a Doctor

1. How can tobacco harm me?
2. How quickly after I start using nicotine could I see negative health effects?
3. In what ways can secondhand smoke harm me?
4. If I already smoke, how can I quit?
5. Have I already done permanent harm to myself by smoking?
6. How much caffeine is too much?
7. How will caffeine affect my long-term health?
8. How can consuming caffeine affect my health now?
9. Why is caffeine worse for children than adults?
10. What's the best way for me to stop using caffeine if I'm already addicted to it?

CHAPTER 4
Policies, Legislation, and Reform

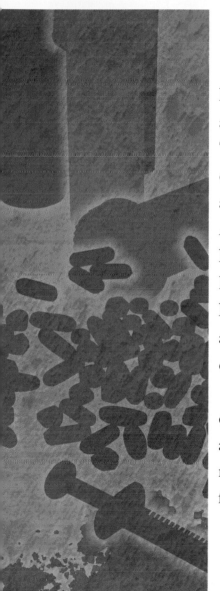

Both caffeine and nicotine are legal substances in the United States. However, though there are many laws regulating the use of nicotine, there are not many laws concerning caffeine. The use of caffeine in sodas has been considered GRAS (Generally Recognized as Safe) by the U.S. Food and Drug Administration (FDA) since 1961, to a limit of 0.02 percent. The FDA does, however, require that caffeine appear on a list of ingredients when it is used as a food additive in things such as soft drinks and caffeinated water.

FDA regulations do not apply to products containing only natural caffeine, like coffee and tea. Furthermore, the FDA also does not require that the quantity of caffeine in food and beverages such as energy drinks

The Food and Drug Administration (FDA) does not require food and beverage companies to disclose the amount of caffeine in their products. However, some companies have decided to voluntarily do so.

be disclosed. However, some companies, like Coca-Cola and PepsiCo, have voluntarily labeled their products with caffeine content. Unlike the caffeine food-labeling requirement, the FDA requires that the quantity of caffeine in over-the-counter drugs, like Vivarin and Excedrine, be disclosed on the drug's label along with warnings regarding caffeine's stimulatory effects.

The American Medical Association and some consumer groups are calling for the mandatory labeling of the quantity of caffeine in foods and beverages. It is especially important for pregnant women to know how much caffeine products contain due to the associated risks of miscarriage, premature birth, and low birth weight. Also, teens drinking energy drinks are at more of a risk of consuming too much caffeine when the drinks are not labeled. A University of Florida study found that even cans of energy drinks that are two-thirds the size of a can of cola can contain two to four times the amount of caffeine. To make things worse, energy drinks are moving to larger and larger cans, increasing the amount of caffeine found in a single can. Kids are consuming cans as large as 24 ounces. A 20-ounce can of Fixx energy drink, for example, contains 500 mg of caffeine. The American Dietetic Association advises adults to consume no more than 300 mg of caffeine per day. Many experts suggest that teens should have no more than 100 mg per day.

Other countries seem to be taking more action than the United States concerning caffeine control. It was suspected that the consumption of energy drinks led to a number of deaths in

Australia, Ireland, and Sweden. As a result, the European Union began requiring energy drinks to carry a health warning about their high content of caffeine in 2004. France and Denmark went as far as to ban the energy drink Red Bull altogether. In 2006, five U.S. governors and seventeen mayors signed proclamations declaring March the National Caffeine Awareness Month to call attention to the dangers of caffeine intoxication.

EARLY CIGARETTE LAWS

People have been attempting to create antismoking laws in America as far back as the 1600s. In the 1890s, twenty-six of the forty-four states in America passed laws prohibiting the sale of cigarettes to minors. Laws making it illegal for minors to smoke in public were also passed. Antismoking groups arose as well. In 1899, Lucy Page Gaston founded the Chicago Anti-Cigarette League. During the early 1900s, states and towns throughout America tried to ban the use of cigarettes by passing laws making it a crime to use or sell them. However, the laws were not enforced and the cigarette prohibition movement died by 1927.

Smoking in America became a real problem. Then, in the 1960s, President John F. Kennedy gave the surgeon general, Dr. Luther Terry, the nation's spokesperson on health, the task of studying the tobacco problem. After a thorough investigation, the surgeon general's report was released on January 11, 1964. It said, "Cigarette smoking is a health hazard of sufficient importance to warrant appropriate remedial action." In 1966, the Federal Cigarette Labeling and Advertising Act was passed, requiring that cigarette packages carry a health warning. In 1970, Congress banned cigarette ads on the radio and television.

PASSIVE (SECONDHAND) SMOKING LAWS

Up until the 1970s, people worried only about how smoking affected smokers. However, in the 1970s, nonsmokers began to complain that smoke from cigarettes smelled, burned their eyes and noses, gave them headaches, and aggravated their allergies. In 1973, Arizona became the first state to restrict smoking in public places. In 1975, legislators in Minnesota passed a Clean Indoor Air Act that provided no-smoking areas inside public buildings for those who did not smoke.

This legislation became a model for other states. However, in the 1970s, not much was known about the health effects of passive smoking, or inhaling someone else's cigarette smoke. The surgeon general, Dr. C. Everett Koop, appointed by President Ronald Regan, provided the information needed to pass more laws concerning passive smoking. Passive smoking was linked to lung cancer and other health issues. In 1979, smoking was restricted in all federal government buildings and was banned completely in the White House in 1993. In 1988, Congress banned smoking on domestic flights that were two hours or

Surgeon General C. Everett Koop attacked the problem of tobacco quite strongly. In 1988, Koop issued a report stating that nicotine is addictive like other drugs such as heroin and cocaine.

fewer, but, by 1990, smoking was not allowed on domestic flights at all. Smoking was allowed on international flights until 1997, when it, too, was banned.

In 2006, the surgeon general sent out a report entitled "Health Consequences of Involuntary Exposure to Tobacco Smoke." This report reaffirmed previous findings that passive smoke causes cancer, heart disease, respiratory problems, and even death. Now, laws in all fifty states and the District of Columbia restrict or ban smoking in certain public areas. States such as New York have passed laws requiring that virtually all indoor facilities, including restaurants and bars, be smoke-free. Studies show that antismoking laws are working. Inspections conducted to determine if New York City is complying with its smoke-free law found that 97 percent of restaurants and bars were not allowing smoking, had posted "No Smoking" signs, and had removed ashtrays.

TOBACCO AND POLITICS

Given what is known about the health issues surrounding tobacco use and the known addictive nature of nicotine, it is astonishing that tobacco is one of the least-regulated products sold in the United States. This is due mainly to the political and economic influence of the tobacco industry. Tobacco companies hire many powerful lobbyists (people who have access to politicians). The industry uses lobbying, the media, public relations, and contributions to politicians to sway votes in favor of tobacco companies, allowing them to sell their products with the least amount of hindrance. Politicians from tobacco-growing states such as Virginia and North Carolina also have the power to affect legislation concerning tobacco. Therefore, tobacco is exempt from virtually every consumer health and safety law enacted by Congress.

In 1996, the FDA claimed control over tobacco products under the Food, Drug, and Cosmetic Act. The FDA regulated the advertising, labeling, and purchasing restrictions of tobacco. However, the tobacco industry sued the federal government, claiming that the FDA lacked the legal authority to regulate them. The U.S. Supreme Court ruled in June 2000 that, in order for the FDA to regulate tobacco, it must first be given legal authority by Congress, which it had not. As a result of this ruling, all of the FDA regulations were dropped, including a federal age minimum for purchase of tobacco (eighteen years old) and federal rules for checking a minor's photo identification.

Currently, the federal government exercises little control over tobacco in the United States. Nearly every other American industry that carries a potential health risk is regulated by a federal agency. This is not so for tobacco companies. However, the federal government has maintained the laws requiring surgeon general warnings and those laws banning television advertising of tobacco products. It is up to the individual states and cities to adopt and enforce clean-air laws and laws concerning the minimum age of tobacco use and the sale of tobacco to minors. In February 2007, two new bills were introduced in Congress that would give the FDA the authority to regulate tobacco.

The Fourteen-Year-Old Lobbyist

In March 1996, a fourteen-year-old girl walked into a government office building and bought cigarettes from a vending machine. She was lobbying in support of the FDA's proposed restrictions on tobacco advertising targeted toward teens. She was also proving that it was too easy for young people to get cigarettes, despite state age restrictions. When she bought the cigarettes, the girl was wearing a T-shirt that read "I am 14 years old."

TOBACCO LAWS AND MINORS

All fifty states in America have laws prohibiting the sale of tobacco to individuals under the age of eighteen. Though this is not a federal law, it is due to the fact that Congress passed the Synar Amendment in 1992, which denies funding to states that do not ban tobacco sales to minors. Federal funds are used by states for things such as fixing roads and building bridges. If states enforce laws that penalize retailers that sell tobacco to minors, it can help to prevent youth from starting to smoke. By enforcing

It is up to individual states, cities, and establishments to decide whether to have smoke-free environments. Some states, like New York, have passed laws banning smoking in almost all indoor facilities.

laws that fine minors for possession of tobacco, states can reduce the cigarette use among minors who already smoke.

Antismoking laws seem to be beneficial for kids, too. Smoke-free policies change the perception that smoking is a normal adult behavior. This has been shown to reduce the number of teens that start using tobacco. A national study found that adolescents are much less likely to become smokers if they work in a smoke-free workplace. A Massachusetts study also found that kids living in towns with smoke-free restaurants were less than half as likely to become smokers as kids living in towns without such laws.

The American Heart Association and many other health organizations would support the legislation that would give the FDA the authority to regulate tobacco. The FDA would have the authority to identify the toxic substances in tobacco products and to require new and larger warning labels on tobacco products. The FDA would also be able to eliminate the advertising, marketing, and availability of tobacco products to children. Many, like the American Heart Association, believe that FDA regulation is critical to reducing the tobacco use of America's youth.

CHAPTER 5

What Is the Impact?

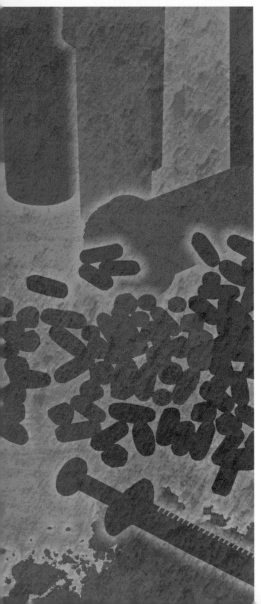

Addiction is a complicated problem that affects not only the health and well-being of addicted people but also their families, friends, and society as a whole. Substance abuse is an expensive public health problem.

When people drink colas and energy drinks, they are not just getting a dose of caffeine. A lot of colas and energy drinks are packed with sugar. The amount of sugar that kids are consuming in soft drinks has been linked to the onset of type 2 diabetes. Type 2 diabetes usually develops in adults who are overweight. However, there has been a sharp increase in the number of cases of type 2 diabetes in children and adolescents in recent years.

Three out of five people who suffer from type 2 diabetes experience

About three hundred thousand deaths in the United States each year are associated with obesity, which is aggravated by the consumption of soft drinks packed with sugar and caffeine.

complications such as heart disease, blindness, kidney damage, and nerve problems. The medical cost of diabetes and its complications in the United States is about one hundred billion dollars annually. In addition to diabetes, caffeine has been directly linked to other medical conditions, like high blood pressure, heart disease, panic and anxiety disorders, infertility, and some cancers. The treatment of all of these problems comes at a cost to the health care system and results in an increased cost of health care as well as of health insurance.

THE COST OF NICOTINE ADDICTION

Tobacco use is the leading preventable cause of death in the United States. The impact of tobacco use on American society in terms of what it costs to treat those who are sick and dying is staggering.

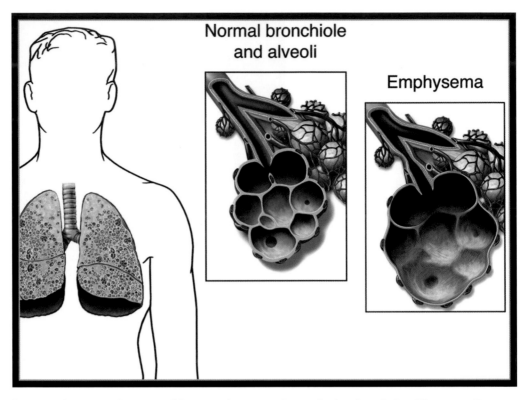

Lungs that are damaged by emphysema lose their elasticity. The small bronchioles collapse, trapping air in the alveoli. The alveoli over-expand and burst.

Smoking is the number one cause of lung cancer, and it is linked to many other cancers as well. Cancer is a very expensive disease to treat. In addition to the chemotherapy and the expensive cancer drugs used to treat the disease, many terminally ill cancer patients require hospice care (care for the terminally ill).

Other costly smoking-related illnesses include heart disease and emphysema. Smoking also generates costs for the treatment of burns caused by smoking-related fires and for the care of premature and low-birth-weight babies of smoking mothers. There are also medical care costs associated with the illnesses caused by passive smoking. Passive smoking is responsible for respiratory problems, heart disease, and even cancer in nonsmokers.

In addition to the health care costs associated with tobacco use, there are also costs to society related to the loss of productivity due to smoking. Smokers are ill much more often than nonsmokers. Absent workers reduce the productivity of companies, thereby increasing the prices of the products they are producing. This is an increased cost to society. Overall, the economic burden caused by tobacco use is estimated to be more than $150 billion a year.

The 1998 Tobacco Master Settlement Agreement

The Tobacco Master Settlement Agreement (MSA) was the largest civil settlement in U.S. history. It resulted from the legal actions brought by forty-six states, the District of Columbia, and five U.S. territories against the tobacco industry. The states sued the tobacco industry for medical costs resulting from smoking-related illnesses. On November 23, 1998, the tobacco industry agreed to pay the states a total of $206 billion through 2025. The MSA also contractually restricted the way tobacco companies advertise, market, and promote tobacco products. Included in the agreement were the banning of youth access to free samples of tobacco products, restrictions on tobacco brand-name sponsorship of events with youth audiences, and the banning of cartoon characters, like Joe Camel, in tobacco advertising.

THE EVERYDAY DRUGS

Because caffeine and nicotine are seen every day in our society, it is tempting to assume that use of them is not dangerous. There is no doubt that both caffeine and nicotine are drugs and that they are addictive. However, "caffeine is where tobacco was 20 years ago," says Laura Juliano, assistant professor in American University's Department of Psychology. Twenty years ago, people were just

Caffeine and nicotine are still accepted in our society. As a result, many people think that they're safe to consume in everyday situations such as working and socializing.

beginning to realize how addictive and dangerous tobacco is. Surgeon General Koop's 1988 report branded nicotine as an addictive substance. However, the tobacco companies fought against his wish to have cigarette warning labels that read: "Surgeon General's Warning: Tobacco Contains Nicotine, an Addictive Drug." The tobacco companies won.

In 2004, the *Seattle Times* reported that Joseph DeRupo, a spokesperson for the National Coffee Association, claimed that caffeine was not addictive. However, many researchers and, for that matter, many coffee drinkers would now disagree. The National Coffee Association reported that 68 percent of people in America admitted last year that they were hooked on coffee. Many have tried and failed to stop drinking coffee.

Like with nicotine, it takes more than a "just quit" attitude to stop using caffeine. Still, not all researchers agree on the degree of caffeine's addictive nature or its health risk. Many still believe that though caffeine is addictive, it is relatively safe when used in moderation. In our society, caffeine is still pushed upon young people with promises of energy and alertness.

Though not as brazen as they once were, tobacco companies are also still targeting the young. Researchers today agree that nicotine in any amount is detrimental to one's health. It will be interesting to see where America stands with caffeine twenty years from now.

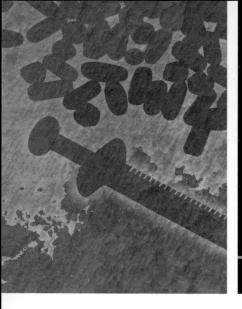

GLOSSARY

addiction A physical or psychological dependence upon a drug.

anxiety A feeling of worry, dread, or uneasiness.

asthma A disease of the respiratory system that causes coughing, difficulty breathing, and tightness in the chest.

bronchitis A lung disease that causes difficulty breathing and severe coughing.

caffeine An addictive drug in some food and drinks that stimulates the central nervous system.

Centers for Disease Control and Prevention (CDC) A government organization responsible for promoting health in America.

dependence A physical or psychological need for something, like a drug.

dip Finely cut or ground tobacco.

drug A substance that changes the way the brain works.

emphysema A lung disease that destroys the flexibility of the lungs, making it difficult to breathe.

Food and Drug Administration (FDA) A federal agency responsible for ensuring that food and drugs are safe, sanitary, and effective.

gateway drug A drug that can lead to the use of other drugs.

lobbyist Someone who tries to influence political policy on a particular issue.

miscarriage The involuntary ending of a pregnancy.

National Institute on Drug Abuse (NIDA) An organization that scientifically examines drug abuse and addiction.

nicotine The addictive component in tobacco that stimulates the central nervous system.

psychoactive Used to describe drugs that have a significant effect on a person's mood or behavior.

snuff Fincly cut tobacco, sometimes drawn into the nose.

stimulant A drug that speeds up the brain and body.

surgeon general The chief public health officer of the United States.

tobacco The plant from which nicotine comes.

tolerance The process by which a person's body becomes used to a drug so that it no longer has the same effect. More and more is needed to get the same effect.

withdrawal The process of the body craving a substance to which it is no longer exposed.

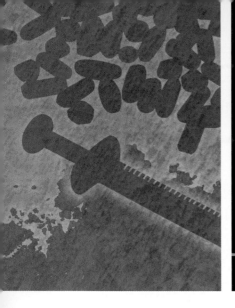

FOR MORE INFORMATION

Food and Drug Administration
5600 Fishers Lane
Rockville, MD 20857
(800) 216-7331
Web site: http://www.fda.gov
The FDA is an organization dedicated to protecting public health by assuring the safety of food and drugs.

Mayo Clinic
4500 San Pablo Road
Jacksonville, FL 32224
(904) 953-2000
Web site: http://www.mayo.edu
The Mayo Clinic is a not-for-profit group that provides answers to questions about drugs, therapies, devices, and treatments.

National Institute on Drug Abuse
National Institutes of Health

6001 Executive Boulevard, Room 5213

Bethesda, MD 20892-9561

(301) 443-1124

Web site: http://www.nida.nih.gov/NIDAHome1.html

The National Institute on Drug Abuse is part of the National Institutes of Health, a component of the U.S. Department of Health and Human Services. It is dedicated to the scientific examination of drug abuse and addiction.

Society for Research on Nicotine and Tobacco

2810 Crossroads Drive, Suite 3800

Madison, WI 53718

(608) 443-2462

Web site: http://www.srnt.org

The Society for Research on Nicotine and Tobacco is dedicated to generating knowledge about nicotine's effects on the body and on society.

WEB SITES

Due to the changing nature of Internet links, Rosen Publishing has developed an online list of Web sites related to the subject of this book. This site is updated regularly. Please use this link to access the list:

http://www.rosenlinks.com/daas/cani

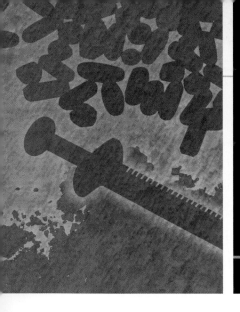

FOR FURTHER READING

Carlson-Berne, Emma. *Nicotine* (History of Drugs). Farmington Hills, MI: Greenhaven Press, 2006.

Connelly, Elizabeth Russell. *Nicotine = Busted!* New York, NY: Enslow Publishers, 2006.

Debenedette, Valerie. *Caffeine* (The Drug Library). New York, NY: Enslow Publishers, 2001.

Mezinski, Pierre, Melissa Daly, and Francoise Jaud. *Drugs Explained.* New York, NY: Amulet Books, 2004.

Moyer, David B., M.D. *The Tobacco Book.* Santa Fe, NM: Sunstone Press, 2005.

Rackley, Jenny. *Nicotine.* Farmington Hills, MI: Lucent Books, 2002.

Wagner, Heather Lehr. *Nicotine* (Drugs: The Straight Facts). New York, NY: Chelsea House, 2003.

Weinberg, Bennett Alan, and Bonnie K. Bealer. *The World of Caffeine: The Science and Culture of the World's Most Popular Drug.* New York, NY: Routledge, 2001.

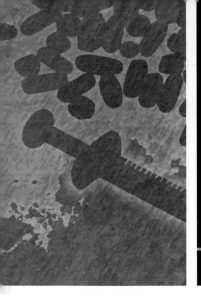

BIBLIOGRAPHY

BBC News. "Red Bull in Suspected Links to Death." July 12, 2001. Retrieved January 5, 2008 (http://news.bbc.co.uk/1/hi/health/1435409.stm).

Farkas A. J., E. A. Gilpin, M. M. White, and J. P. Pierce. "Association Between Household and Workplace Smoking Restrictions and Adolescent Smoking." *Journal of the American Medical Association*, 284(6), 2000, pp. 717–722.

Henderson, Elizabeth Connell. *Understanding Addiction.* Jackson, MS: University Press of Mississippi, 2000.

Hirschfelder, Arlene. *Kick Butts: A Kid's Guide to a Tobacco-Free America.* New York, NY: Julian Messner, 1998.

Hughes, J. R., D. K. Hatsukami, J. E. Mitchel, and L A. Dahlgren. "Prevalence of Smoking Among Psychiatric Outpatients." *American Journal of Psychiatry*, 143, 1986, pp. 993–997.

McCuen, Gary E. *Tobacco: People, Profits, and Public Health.* Hudson, WI: Gary E. McCuen Publications, Inc, 1997.

Medical News Today. "French Ban on Red Bull (Drink) Upheld by European Court." Retrieved January 28, 2008 (www.medicalnewstoday.com/index.php?newsid=5753).

Shaffer, H. J. "Addictive Personality." *Encyclopedia of Psychology.* Washington, DC: American Psychological Association and Oxford University Press, 2000.

Siegel M., A. B. Albers, D. M. Cheng, L. Biener, and N. A. Rigotti. "Effect of Local Restaurant Smoking Regulations on Progression to Established Smoking Among Youths." *Tobacco Control*, 4(5), 2005, pp. 300–306.

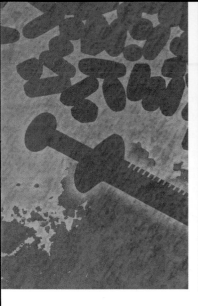

INDEX

ABOUT THE AUTHOR

Heather Elizabeth Hasan graduated from college summa cum laude with a dual major in chemistry and biochemistry. She attributes the fact that she never used tobacco to the influence and early education she received about smoking from her parents. She has two small children, Samuel and Matthew, with whom she is already discussing the dangers of drug use.

PHOTO CREDITS

P. 5 Ralph Orlowski/Getty Images; p. 8 Daniele Pellegrini/Getty Images; p. 11 Baerbel Schmidt/Getty Images; p. 13 Private Collection/Bridgeman Art Library; pp. 15, 18, 40, 44 © AP Images; p. 21 © Pascal Goetgheluck/ Photo Researchers; p. 24 © www.istockphoto.com/Eric Simard; p. 26 © Richard Levine/Alamy; p. 30 Taxi/Getty Images; p. 32 Peter Cade/ Iconica/Getty Images; p. 35 Library of Congress Prints and Photographs Division; p. 48 Tim Boyle/Getty Images; p. 51 © Chet Gordon/The Image Works; p. 52 Illustration © 2008 Nucleus Medical Art. All rights reserved. www.nucleusinc.com; p. 54 © Bob Daemmrich/The Image Works.

Designer: Tahara Anderson; Editor: Nicholas Croce
Photo Researcher: Amy Feinberg